MICHAEL LANDON

Life, Love & Laughter

A TRIBUTE TO A BELOVED ACTOR
BY THE PEOPLE WHO KNEW HIM BEST

BY HARRY FLYNN AND PAMELA FLYNN

PHOTOGRAPHY BY
GENE TRINDL

FOREWORD BY
CINDY LANDON

POMEGRANATE PRESS, LTD.

This is a Pomegranate Press, Ltd. book.

MICHAEL LANDON: Life, Love & Laughter
Text copyright by Harry Flynn and Pamela Flynn.
Photographs copyright by Gene Trindl.
Published 1991 by Pomegranate Press, Ltd., Post Office Box 8261,
Universal City, California 91608–0261.

The text was set in Adobe® Stone Informal, and was printed and
bound in the United States of America by McNaughton & Gunn, Inc.,
Ann Arbor, Michigan.
10 9 8 7 6 5 4 3 2

Library of Congress Catalog Card Number: 91-75319
Hardcover Edition ISBN: 0-938817-31-0
Tradepaper Edition ISBN: 0-938817-29-9

For Pomegranate Press, Ltd:
Editor: Kathryn Leigh Scott
Book Design: Ben Martin
Book Cover Design: Heidi Frieder
Copy Editor: Gina Renée Gross
Composition Consultant: Leroy Chen

This book is dedicated to the man who brought out the best in all of us,
MICHAEL LANDON

Foreword

Michael brought joy to so many millions of people who watched his television shows. He brought a special joy to those who were privileged to know him personally. His contagious laugh and slightly off-center humor got all of us through the roughest of times with a smile.

He loved to laugh. He loved to make others laugh, and as serious as any of Michael's shows might have been, shooting them, as you will see, was pure pleasure for everyone who worked with him. He brought that wonderful sense of humor to everything he did.

Michael was an extraordinary human being. He created love, laughter, and inspiration for all of us who knew and loved him. I hope these pictures and stories will help keep that legacy alive. He will be greatly missed by all of us, but what he stood for will never die, and will always remain in our hearts.

Cindy Landon

Acknowledgments

We gratefully acknowledge the kind and generous assistance of Jim Adlhock, Army Archerd, Ed Asner, Lew Ayres, Barbara Barry, Marilyn Beck, Haskell "Buzzy" Boggs, Ernest Borgnine, Hank Brissinger, Hal Burton, Art Carney, Johnny Carson, Bill Claxton, Marvin Coil, Ron Cooper, Robin Dearden, Dick DeNeut, Maury Dexter, Michael Donaldson, David Dortort, Marianne Dunlop, Pepper Edmiston, Susan Edwards, Jay Eller, Judith Farkas, Andy Fenady, Maureen Flannigan, Daniel Forge, Ruth "Foss" Foster, Eddie Foy III, Doug Friedman, Paula Gibbs, Timothy Gibbs, Patty Gibson, Dan Gordon, Moses Gunn, Vince Gutierrez, Clyde Harper, Helen Hayes, Bob Hope, Darby Hoppin, Ron Housiaux, Tom Ito, Ann Jackson, Andrea Jaffe, Ron Janoff, James Karen, Bill Kiley, Vickie King, Dennis Korn, David Kramer, Frances Labyorteaux, Matthew Labyorteaux, Patrick Labyorteaux, Ron Labyorteaux, Cheryl Landon, Cindy Landon, Mark Landon, Herm Lewis, Barbera Libis, Dick Lilley, John Loeffler, A.C. Lyles, Todd Margoluis, Barney Martin, Doug McClure, Joyce McConnell, Kent McCray, Susan McCray, Juliette McGrew, Joan McKenna, Bobby Miles, Jan Morrill, Richard Mulligan, Brianne Murphy, Julian Myers, Patricia Neal, Leslie Nielsen, Jill Olsen, Merlin Olsen, Ian Pearl, Susan Pearl, Casey Peterson, Nancy Reagan, Pam Roylance, Arnold Shapiro, Bill Sheehan, Brooke Shields, Bill Shotland, Steve Sohmer, Whitey Snyder, Jeff Sotzing, Tom Sullivan, Lisa Sweeney, Shan Tabor, Ralph Taeger, Brandon Tartikoff, Jerry Taylor, Mike Termini, Cleo Terrio, Jim Troesh, Dick Van Dyke, Nick Venet, Debbie Vickers, Evy Wagner, Eli Wallach, John Warren, Erika Wernher, Betty White, Jack Willingham, Dean Wilson, Gary Wohlleben, Josh Wood, and Brad Yacobian.

Introduction

We were very privileged to work with Michael Landon for almost nine years, and this book is an attempt to share the joy it was to know the man. He was a genius on a sound stage, but he was also great fun to be around.

He possessed a wicked sense of humor. He loved practical jokes, even when they were played on him. He shared the latest funny stories with everyone in earshot, and he never failed to find a humorous side to any situation.

When he was very ill at the end of a brilliant life, he was still finding the humor in every event, even the sadder ones. He called me over while the cameras were still rolling during his final press conference, saying with a huge grin, "Harry, come here. Next to you I still look husky."

At one point we spoke on the phone. I said, "But Michael, you sound great." "It's not my voice that's sick, Harry," he responded.

He evoked strong emotions in all his friends and co-workers. These are their memories, some sweet, some funny. They'll touch you as they did us.

This is my favorite picture with Michael. It is a perfect example of the little boy at play. And at heart he was always that little boy, finding youthful happiness to make up for a childhood devoid of it.

We did a show about a girl with a weight problem, and the pie was a prop. He caught me totally unaware, but he had tipped Gene Trindl, the unit photographer, to be prepared. Gene got it all. My surprise and Michael's delight. That's the Michael we knew.

He told Linda Taylor, our costumer, to make sure I got a new suit, but I wouldn't. I had the pie suit cleaned and it hung in the closet, just in case he ever got the notion to repeat the incident. I didn't wear it again until the day of Mike's memorial. I figured wherever he was, he'd appreciate it.

Harry Flynn

Life

Michael always said that the day after "Bonanza" debuted in 1959 people suddenly found him inches taller and ten times sexier. I doubt if he could have been any funnier. A sense of humor like his is something you're born with. Michael relished humor that didn't hurt anyone, and he loved a laugh at his own expense. If you were on his crew you were part of the family, and if you were part of the family, then you probably got kidded. It was when he didn't kid you that you worried.

Jay Eller was Michael's business manager and his friend for over thirty years. They were opposites in many ways; Michael was casual, Jay was mercilessly formal. But they shared a brightness, a sharper perception of the world than many of their peers, and Jay learned to appreciate Michael's humor. In his eulogy at the memorial service, Jay mentioned that when someone asked Mike about the possibility of losing his hair due to chemotherapy he replied, "I'm rich. I'll buy a hat!"

Michael also predicted that he'd still be cover-boy material for magazines even if he were bald. "There's always *Bowlers' Monthly*," he said.

Michael and Cindy loved animals and Jay mentioned one particular pet, a 13-year-old lap dog named Lucy. She had always driven him crazy, and now she was really annoying him by just being there. "That little sucker's going to outlive me!"

He truly loved to laugh. Anyone who watched him in interviews, such as on Johnny Carson's "Tonight Show," remembers his laugh—rich, full, contagious, and unique to Michael. You could pick it out of a crowd.

Life started out without any laughs at all for Michael, who grew up as Eugene Orowitz, an Irish-Catholic Jewish kid from Collingswood, New Jersey. He was caught in the middle of his parents' strange marriage where neither partner talked to the other for weeks on end. As a youngster, Mike found a hideout for himself in a cave-like excavation where he would conceal canned goods against the time when he would leave home for good. The earlier years must have been devastating for the boy—when your folks don't love you, what else is there?

Once he gained stardom they came out of the woodwork, but as a skinny little kid in Jersey, Michael had few friends. As only one of two Jewish kids in the whole high school, he was in fights all the time, and he rebelled against any and all authority. And, although he was a brilliant student, he intentionally failed all his classes.

A large measure of Mike's problems as a youngster was due to the intolerable situation at home. Mrs. Orowitz, a former actress named Peggy O'Neill, constantly tried to commit suicide, but never with a serious intent. A volatile and highly unstable woman, his mother would hail a taxicab and set out in her nightgown to find her son. Once she'd found him, even if he were among classmates, she would physically pull him into the cab and take him back home. Somehow the incredible funny bone he was born with kept him laughing through the tears. About his suicide-prone mother, he joked, "I was ten before I knew you put anything but a head into a gas oven."

❖

The bruises from this troubled childhood left their marks. Although his father was a somewhat remote man, Michael felt closer to him. His dad had been very successful in New York, working for Paramount Studios as a publicist, doing radio work, and writing for newspapers and magazines. When Michael came to the West Coast his father followed. He thought he could find work among all his old friends in the movie industry.

One of the most poignant stories Michael told is about the time he drove his dad to Paramount Studios and parked outside the De Mille Gate on Marathon Street while his father went to find an old friend or two on the lot. He expected a warm welcome. Michael waited in the car. His father walked up to the gate to announce himself. It was a disaster. None of the executives he asked for remembered him. His humiliation in front of his son was devastating. Michael, who cared deeply for his father, suffered the pain intensely.

At the time, he couldn't do anything about it. Later, when his enormous success made him a welcome visitor to any studio lot in Hollywood, Eli was gone. The memory hurt him, but those experiences fueled his vivid imagination and instilled a desire to create family television shows with positive, caring environments.

When Michael was seventeen his life took a new direction. He threw a javelin for the first time—and threw it farther than anyone else on the Collingswood High School

Above. Landon directs Timothy Patrick Murphy as Eugene Orowitz in *Sam's Son*. Below left. His mother Peggy O'Neill with his sister Vickie in a 1959 photo. Below right is his father Eli, who died just before his son gained fame in *Bonanza*

track team. The lonely kid with the battered self-esteem had found a skill that set him apart and gave him a chance to excel.

Michael recreated this episode of his life in the picture *Sam's Son* that he produced in 1983. Eli Wallach played his dad.

"I used to tease him about his curly locks," Eli recalls. "Staring at my balding white head, he'd say, 'I'll lend you some of my hair...but not for long.'"

Mike with Eli Wallach and Victor French clowning in front of a World War II vintage Air Force B-25 bomber used in an episode of "Highway to Heaven"

Michael said that when Eli appeared on the set in a black fedora like the one his dad had always worn, tears came to his eyes. He felt close to his dad, despite the poor communication between father and son. Michael was frustrated by the fact that his greatest achievement as a youth—throwing the javelin—made no sense to the elder Orowitz at all. Mike said when his dad came to watch, he'd stand outside the fence around the track stadium, watch Michael throw, then shake his head and leave. He was pleased that his son won competitions, but the sport itself was meaningless to him. Throwing spears, said his father, was for guys hunting supper in the jungle.

Michael first arrived in Los Angeles as a college-bound teenager. His skill throwing the javelin had earned him a track scholarship at USC. While his sister Vickie, who had represented New Jersey in the Long Beach Miss Universe contest, pursued an acting career, young Michael enrolled as a college student and pursued athletics. At a time when crew-cuts were all the rage, Michael sported longer hair than was popular on campus. During his freshman year, a group of football players held Landon down and clipped his overly long locks. A fairly ordinary prank among college boys, the occasion marked another turn in Michael's life. He had come to believe in the Sampson legend, that long hair gave him strength and when it was cut he was shorn of his power. Whatever the truth of the legend, Michael never again threw the javelin with his former prowess. Within months of the haircutting incident, Eugene Orowitz of Collingswood, New Jersey, was relieved of his USC scholarship, and consequently forfeited his academic status.

He went to work to earn a living, taking a job as a laborer at the Kress Department Store warehouse. One day he visited his sister and her friend David Kramer, then a fellow acting student and today a well-known Hollywood writer and public relations consultant. The two were rehearsing a scene for their workshop with Estelle Harmon, the legendary acting coach. The story goes that Michael kidded them so much about their effete pursuit that they challenged him to try his hand at acting. He auditioned for the class, and was immediately given a scholarship.

Later, agent Bob Raison took him on and suggested he change his name. Jewish surnames weren't as much in evidence on the Hollywood rosters those days. They agreed on Michael as his first name and Mike chose Landon out of the phone book, although Raison had suggested London. To Mike, "Landon" was more informal.

Nick Venet met Michael in the mid-fifties when they were both living in a low-rent Victorian-style apartment building in the seedier side of Hollywood. Michael was trying to make ends meet any way he could until he found acting work. Nick was trying to carve a trail to success in the music business. They were both still in their teens. Michael, his first wife Dody, and their son Mark, whom Michael had adopted, lived downstairs; Nick lived upstairs. When Mike woke up in the morning, he would poke his javelin, a last vestige of his USC career, at the ceiling to wake up Nick.

One morning the old floors could resist no longer and the point of the javelin went through the ceiling into Nick's bedroom. It stayed stuck through Nick's floor until they moved.

At the time, Michael was selling blankets door to door because the flexible hours gave him time to go out on calls for acting jobs. Mike's dad came out to visit him and, after being rebuffed by the studios, found work managing the Rialto Theater on

Record producer Nick Venet at the recording console,
photographed by Michael Landon in 1963

Landon and his crew filming on location

Western Avenue. Nick and Mike worked for him in the evenings, and they would bring their starving actor friends in the side door to watch the current flick for free.

All of them were avid students of film, so it was more than a frivolous gesture. It backfired when Mr. Orowitz discovered that the orchestra seats held only four patrons one quiet night, while the balcony had the first three rows filled with people. Something was fishy. He fired Nick on the spot, and then later relented, saying, "Why didn't you tell me? I would have let you—it's for a good cause." The kicker for Nick was that he discovered his buddy was charging the starving actors fifty cents a head!

They shared almost everything in those early years, including Michael's old Cadillac (bought from Hedda Hopper's son, Bill), and a pair of black leather shoes found in a thrift store. When they each had interviews on the same day, the one with the first interview wore the leather shoes, while the other wore sneakers. They would exchange footwear between interviews.

Nick found that the Landons were the soul of generosity, even when none of them had a dime. He ate with them, and they all shared what they had. Therefore, Nick's big break as an actor became a windfall for all of them. It started when Mike came home one day glowing with excitement. The series "Broken Arrow" was shooting on the old Fox Western Studios lot just down the street. Mike had talked them into auditioning a real Indian friend of his. Nick.

"So?" Nick asked. "I'm Greek!"

"So now you're an Indian," Mike said. "Just come with me and don't say anything. I'll be your interpreter."

And he did. Nick played an Indian on the show, and never spoke any English at all, while Mike was his interpreter. They paid Nick fifteen hundred dollars for the week, more than any of them had ever seen at one time, and they got ahead in the rent for two months for both apartments.

But Nick still shakes his head. "Who but Michael could have pulled it off?"

While waiting for a break, Nick and Michael hung around with friends from their acting classes, all of them ambitious actors such as Steve McQueen, Rafael Camos, Sal Mineo, and Corey Allen. Along the way, Nick got a job as associate producer at the Players Ring Theater in Hollywood. Rod Amateau, who two years later began producing and directing "Dobie Gillis" for CBS, was directing the play "Tea and Sympathy." Nick read some of the script and suggested to Michael that he audition for a role. In retrospect, Michael wouldn't appear to be suitable casting. The play is about a very ivy league youth, raised with great wealth and class, who is homosexual.

Nevertheless, Michael got the part, and he received great notices. All of a sudden, agents started calling and casting people were interested in him. He got his first acting job on a TV show, John Nesbitt's "Passing Parade," and was on his way to building a remarkable career in Hollywood.

Michael got his start in television during the golden age of live broadcast in the fifties. He worked on "Playhouse 90" several times, and appeared in one of those dramas with Warren Beatty. The two had a great time during rehearsals, but hanging over them in those pre-tape days was the specter of performing live. Fine, if you're cool and in control, but Landon and Beatty both got the giggles during dress rehearsal. Every time they looked at each other they would break up. They managed to avoid each other until air time, and then desperately tried not to be in each other's line of sight. When the crucial scene came up between the two of them, Michael said they were tight as bow strings and barely pulled it off without cracking up.

David Dortort wrote the pilot for "Bonanza" and produced the series. Dan Blocker, Lorne Greene, and Michael had appeared in another show Dortort produced starring John Payne called "Restless Gun," so he knew three of the four leads he wanted for "Bonanza." Dortort would be very instrumental in Michael's early career.

Ralph Taeger was star of a show called "Hondo" in the early sixties, and he and Michael worked out together in the Paramount gym. Ralph recalls how much the other stars of westerns on television envied Michael's ability to control his own career. Everyone wanted to write, direct, and take charge of his or her own destiny, but "Michael was the one who did it. Nobody else did."

Taeger says that Michael trained with a boxer named Joey Indrasano and worked out with the heavy punching bag, "but while there was terrific respect for Michael's prowess with his fists, there was even greater admiration for the heights he scaled as a creative member of the Hollywood community."

Steve McQueen, a long-time friend of Michael's, also worked out in the Paramount Gym. McQueen didn't understand why Michael worked so hard trying to sell his writing and become a director. "What's he want to do, control it all?"

The answer was yes. And for good reason. Michael said in interviews many times, that he knew an actor worked when a producer wanted him to work. But as an actor who was also his own producer, he would work all the time.

Dortort remembers one Friday evening when the company finished filming an episode and had to close down production until they could write a new script. Everyone else looked for something to do to occupy time during what loomed as an instant vacation. But not Michael. He went home and worked out a story idea for an episode and brought it in to Dortort. It was written in longhand, on yellow pads, and it was

Mike, Dan, Lorne, and Pernell with "Bonanza" producer David Dortort

thirty-eight pages long. "I said it should be longer and Michael told me I could fill in the rest. It was rough, but the storyline was good and together we worked on it over the weekend." By the following Wednesday there was a shooting script, and Michael had his first writing credit.

Getting a directing assignment was tougher, but Michael waited for his opportunity. During a big press conference with the actors and producers, Dortort was asked if any of the stars of the series would direct episodes. "Sure, they will," Dortort replied.

"When?" asked Michael.

"Soon," said Dortort, with apprehension.

"Soon when?" persisted Michael.

By now the press was picking up on the challenge. Everyone waited for the producer's

reply. "I have to see what episode hasn't already been assigned to a director," Dortort said.

"Well, Number 17 has no director assigned," said Michael. He'd sprung the trap. David knew it—and there was no denying this young Turk with a tiger in his tank.

David assented gracefully. "It's yours," he told the eager Landon. With his third hat imminent, "I called him the triple-threat," Dortort recalled. "And he was."

As one of the legendary Cartwrights on "Bonanza," Michael became a folk hero of immense proportions. He was the heartthrob of the family group, and, as such, garnered an amazing amount of fan mail—and incredible power for a young actor. But he was always loyal to the group, and looked out for the interests of the other members of the Ponderosa family.

One year, soon after "Bonanza" began to be a huge hit, the network tried to economize on the cast salaries. The actors went together to the annual meeting with the powers that be, and they were presented with a flat statement: no salary increase. Michael, who was easily recognized as the one with the star power, could have asked for separate negotiations, but it would not have occurred to him. No one moved, and no one spoke. Michael calmly got up, grabbed his coat, and walked toward the door.

"Go ahead you guys, whatever you want," he told his fellow actors. "I won't work without a raise." He got as far as the corridor.

It doesn't take a pocket calculator to figure out how many seconds it took for the network brass to trot after him, explaining it had all been a terrible mistake. The Cartwrights got their raises and returned to the Ponderosa.

Dortort hired another director to back Michael in case he needed a hand. That director was Bill Claxton, who eventually directed more "Bonanza," "Little House on the Prairie," and "Father Murphy" episodes than anyone else aside from Michael. Mike never forgot who helped him through that first directorial assignment on "Bonanza."

It was Bill who taught young Landon flexibility as a director. Desert scenery was required for an episode of "Bonanza," but as they began shooting on location in Arizona, it began to rain. It rained steadily throughout the entire schedule and each night the script was rewritten to accommodate the downpour. The skies cleared, however, on the final day when portions of scenes in which rain had already been established had to be completed with close-ups of Michael. A water truck was hired, but it broke down on the way to the location. Claxton and producer Kent McCray decided to hook a hose to the reserve tanks of the honeywagon truck, which housed the rest rooms, to pump water that would simulate rain. The cameras rolled for

Mike, in twenties costume as writer Jack London, and producer Andy Fenady scouting locations on the waterfront and at Jack London Square in Oakland, California

Michael's close-up, but halfway through the take he stopped and said, "If there are any more lumps in this rain, McCray, you'll be sorry!"

Acting, directing, and starring in "Bonanza" prepared Michael to assume the reins of his own series. When "Bonanza" ended, he began to scout around for properties he could call his own. Ed Friendly had bought the Laura Ingalls Wilder books for three thousand dollars—a purchase that ultimately earned the producer over twenty million dollars. He wanted Michael to co-produce and star in the series, but Michael decided he would do it only if he could produce the show entirely on his own. Friendly had no objection to stepping out of the producer's spot if he could split the profits, and that's the way they agreed to handle it. Michael took over as sole executive producer. Ed stepped aside and got rich. The rest, as they say, is history.

About the same time, producer Andy Fenady came back into Michael's life. They first met when they worked out together at the Paramount Studios gym. Andy had produced Nick Adams' series, "The Rebel," and Michael and Nick were friends. When "Bonanza" ended, Andy had an idea that Mike might be perfect casting for a series based on the novelist-adventurer Jack London. Mike liked the idea. Once "Bonanza" was finished, Mike, Andy, and photographer Herm Lewis went to Oakland, California, and shot some portraits of Michael. Dressed in twenties period wardrobe and photographed on locations around the Oakland docks, Mike fit right into the role. He was Jack London, writer, adventurer.

However, Mike had to tell Andy that he was committed to do "Little House," and he couldn't film another pilot while that show was on the network schedule.

"What's it about?" Fenady asked. Mike told him.

"A family on the frontier?" Andy snorted. "No problem. We'll do Jack London next year."

Eleven years later, "Little House" wrapped its final episode.

Love

Kent McCray was Michael's best friend and producing partner for almost thirty years. To interpret the creative genius of a Michael Landon, it took the managerial magic of a Kent McCray, but their relationship got off to a rocky start. Kent joined "Bonanza" in 1962 after a long stint as a production manager on numerous NBC shows, including Bob Hope's specials. It was McCray's first day on the job and the "Bonanza" company was shooting in Vasquez Rocks in the Santa Susannah Mountains, a traditional location spot for western shows, about twenty miles outside of Hollywood. McCray and Landon did not know one another.

The day was hot and Michael had been working hard high up in the rocks. When he came down from his sweltering perch, he walked up to Kent and said, "You better have a car ready for me at one o'clock, 'cause I'm leaving.' "

Kent looked at the schedule, and thought,"Hell, he's in every scene this afternoon." Kent phoned the office and no one there knew anything about Mike doing publicity or promotional calls for NBC. He was not scheduled to be anywhere except on location. Kent wasn't used to taking guff from any actor, so the beefy McCray looked around for Landon and found the actor still in a surly mood."You got my car?" he asked.

"No, and you're not going to get one."

"Well, I'm leaving," Landon told him.

"Well, it's a long, goddamn walk back to Los Angeles," McCray said.

"Yeah?"

"Yeah. And if you leave before I let you go I'm going to sue you and take you to the Guild and you won't even get paid for this week. How do you like that?"

"I don't like it."

Mike and producer Kent McCray

Mike with casting director Susan Sukman McCray

"What are you going to do about it?"

"Well, I guess I'm going to work."

And thus began a lasting relationship that culminated in Mike telling Cindy just days before he died, "Kent was my brother."

❖

Susan Sukman McCray was Michael's casting director for almost two decades, and is married to his producing partner, Kent McCray. The threesome were very close and many mornings the McCrays would drive their director/producer/writer/star to the studio.

As with everything else Michael produced and directed, he had final approval on every detail of production, including casting. However, when Susan cast "The Loneliest Runner" in 1976, he gave her authority to hire actors for some of the smaller parts without auditioning them himself. His trust in Sue was certainly merited. She had been a part of the Landon troupe through most of "Bonanza," cast "Little House," and remained with his production team throughout the rest of his career.

But it happened that one of the actors she cast in a minor role didn't quite work out. When Sue watched the dailies, her mistake was immediately evident. The line reading was painfully bad, and Sue responded by coughing whenever the actor spoke. When the picture went to rough cut, Sue sat through the screening with Mike, and again she coughed at the line. Not a word from the boss. Landon appeared to be too busy checking other matters. During the screening of the first trial answer print, Sue coughed again. Still no comment from Michael. When the show went on the air, it earned high ratings and great critical acclaim—and Sue never heard a word about her "mistake."

Seventeen years, and many Michael Landon productions later, Sue was preparing to cast Michael's brilliant NBC film "Where Pigeons Go to Die." Michael had agreed with her that the smaller parts could be cast locally in Lawrence, Kansas, but he added, "Cast me somebody you don't have to cough through!"

❖

The ease with which Michael placed new people in comfortable situations on the sets he directed made a host of guest stars speak glowingly of the Landon experience, among them Ned Beatty, who appeared in two "Highway to Heaven" episodes. Michael readily agreed when guest star Ed Asner mentioned a change in blocking, although altering the movements meant taking the time to re-light the set. "I've never seen

Ned Beatty

Richard Mulligan

Mike, on location for "Highway," directing Ned Beatty and Victor French

Landon with Ed Asner

anything like the respect he had for actors," said Asner. Richard Mulligan, pre-"Empty Nest," played a newspaper reporter trying to find the truth about Christmas in "Bassinger's New York." "From the moment we met, we were friends...a darlin' man!" says Mulligan.

Art Carney had always been a great idol to Michael, and when the actor agreed to do the TV movie "Where Pigeons Go to Die," Michael was filled with both anxiety and delight. However, Michael need not have been concerned about how Carney would respond to him—they got along famously. Art loved working for Michael. On the first day of filming, he told an interviewer, "Why did I come to Kansas to do this picture? I'll give you the answer in two words: Michael Landon!"

At the beginning of the shoot, Carney would remain on the set, but as he got more comfortable he'd wait in his motor home. Whenever it was time for Art to appear in front of the cameras, Michael himself would wander over to the door of Art's dressing room and, in his best Gleason imitation, bellow, "Norton, get out here!"

And Art would respond in his Norton voice, and come out in a Norton walk, and the crew loved it.

At the end of the Kansas shoot, when Art was set to leave for his home on the East Coast the following morning, Michael slipped a note under his hotel room door:

> *Dear Art,*
>
> *Working with you has been one of the most memorable experiences of my life. I so wanted you to be the man I had enjoyed all those years. You were that man and more. You are an amazingly honest actor, and a joy to be with every moment.*
>
> *Michael*

Carney treasures the note.

❖

On the plains outside of Tucson, Arizona, Michael filmed a "Highway" episode about the orphan mustangs that roam the western prairies. He invited an old friend, stunt rider Richard Farnsworth, who had gone on to become an Academy Award-winning actor, to guest star. Farnsworth was at home among the cowboy stuntmen assembled for the episode, all of whom spun tales with Michael and Victor French about the heyday of television westerns in the sixties. One of Michael's happiest moments

Art Carney and Landon

Landon, Richard Farnsworth, and Gail Strickland

Landon, Victor French, and Ernest Borgnine

was attending the Golden Boot awards with Cindy one year, and receiving an award from Victor.

Ernest Borgnine was a guest star on "Little House," and became a fan of Michael's immediately. On the set, the five-times-married Borgnine took a lot of ribbing from Michael. One day a friend of Mike's happened to come by and see the Oscar-winning actor in Darby Hoppin's makeup chair. They started to shake hands when Michael warned, "If you touch him he's liable to marry you."

While they were working one day, Ernie noticed a large American Flag in an antique store, with a legend indicating that it had once flown over the Mare Island Naval Station. Ernie told Mike that he had been stationed there in the navy during the forties, and that because this flag had only forty-eight stars, it probably dated from the time he did his hitch. Michael took note.

During the cast party at the end of the week's shooting, Michael presented Ernie with the flag that now hangs in his home. When he's asked if the navy awarded him the flag, he says, "Even better, Michael Landon."

The power of television is always amazing, and Michael's command of it was exceptional. It was no surprise that when "Little House" ended it's phenomenal run with an episode that blew up the town of Walnut Grove, there were strong reactions from the television audience.

James Karen, a well-known character actor, played the person who ordered Walnut Grove residents out of their town. He became the man "who destroyed Walnut Grove," and received a lot of hate mail. Trouble was, the hate mail didn't go to him, it went to Pathmark Stores. James had been "Mr. Pathmark" in their TV commercials for eighteen years. The store officials and the ad agency execs were very nervous. Their symbol had been sullied. What to do?

James had worked for Michael the year before playing the high school principal in his feature film, *Sam's Son*. Michael knew him well and was willing to help save his image. At the Landon office, Jim and Michael shared a peace pipe and a picture of the event was spread far and wide by the media. Everyone at Pathmark in New York breathed easier.

James Karen has now been Mr. Pathmark for twenty-two years.

James Karen and Mike smoke a peace pipe for the news media

Cinematographer Bri Murphy reads her light meter on the set before filming

Hank Brissinger, Erika Wernher, and Bill Sheehan

Brianne Murphy is still Hollywood's only female director of photography in the prestigious ASC—and cracking into the union did not come easily. Legend has it that the local's business agent told her she would attain membership in the all-male union, "over my dead body." The day he died, Bri showed up at the business office and declared, "He promised me." She got in. Bri worshipped Michael. "He was a genius," she says of her mentor, and adored his lighter side.

While on location in Arizona, Michael and Bri found themselves riding in a crowded elevator to the twentieth floor of a downtown Tucson building. Michael sensed that the other passengers were awed by his presence. They had traveled several floors in hushed silence before Michael said to Brianne, "Bri, honey, let's step to the front in case anyone farts."

Yet the light-hearted Landon showed compassion and sensitivity when Bri told Michael and Kent McCray that she had to take time off from "Father Murphy" for breast cancer surgery. As she recalls it, "To any other producing team in Hollywood this would have been all the reason necessary to get a new, healthier director of photography. Michael just asked, 'When can we hope to get you back?'" Bri credits her rapid recovery to that generous support.

❖

Erika Wernher, a script supervisor on "Highway," came to the show with impeccable credentials, having worked with such luminaries as Howard Hawks and Mervyn Leroy. According to grip Cleo Terrio, even the decorous and stylish script supervisor could not escape the constant clowning that surrounded any Michael Landon production.

One morning Ron Housiaux, a long-standing member of Michael's crew-family, gently tapped Erika on her behind.

"Get out of here, you pervert," she barked at him, in a convivial early morning greeting. Housiaux, taking it in fun, found every opportunity to sidle up and gently caress Erika's backside.

Erika, however, found the joke wearing thin and became quite furious. Finally she'd had enough, and at the next gentle pat she turned and shouted, "Stop that, you little...Oh, Michael, it's you." Erika turned beet red. "I thought it was that damned Housiaux."

Michael looked distressed. "Erika, love, I thought you knew my touch!"

Cinematographer Haskell "Buzzy" Boggs

Haskell "Buzzy" Boggs has been a cinematographer for over half a century, having begun his career at Paramount in the thirties. In 1959, he became the director of photography on a new show called "Bonanza," and that initiated a long and dedicated relationship with one of the show's stars. When Michael shot his last show, the pilot for "US," in January 1991, Buzzy was the cinematographer, and he was then a man pushing eighty-three.

When his wife became ill in 1985, Buzzy retired to be with her. Two years later she died, and Buzzy was very depressed by her death. He told the mortuary to prepare for a small funeral, as there wouldn't be many mourners. Michael and Kent heard about Mrs. Boggs' death, and on the day of the funeral they closed the set so the company could go to the small chapel to pay their respects. Buzzy was very touched.

After the funeral, Kent and Michael began calling Buzzy, urging him to come back to work. Buzzy was reluctant; he thought he was too old. But they insisted. Finally Buzzy agreed, but on one condition: "It has to be fun," he told Michael. Mike promised it would be.

❖

Michael, who cared deeply about environmental issues, frequently wove his concerns about conservation into his shows. In the "Birds of a Feather" episode of "Highway," Michael wore a bird suit to illustrate the plight of birds dying of pollution. In filming the episode, Michael and his crew had to deal with a host of environmental pollution problems of their own. The costume, made from real bird feathers, was hot and uncomfortable to wear, particularly when Michael had to ride a bicycle in his role. The strong solvents used to clean the feathers caused them to drop off, and costumer Mike Termini, who designed the suit, had to glue them back on with spray glue. The glue smell nearly caused Michael and his stand-in, Dick Lilley, to pass out. Further-more, to avoid sacrificing animals for filming, the prop men had acquired birds that had died accidentally. As the day wore on, the less-than-fresh birds began to fowl the air. Passersby found it intriguing to watch a man wearing a bird suit directing. Nevertheless, the show was a powerful statement and brought praise from environ-mentalists everywhere.

❖

Michael was known for his straightforwardness and honesty, and his shows always reflected those qualities. When NBC approached him to include a little more action on "Little House," maybe some pioneer violence, Michael flatly refused.

Landon directing in the bird suit with Kenny Hunter and Ted Voightlander

Landon directing co-star Victor French

Occasionally he found himself standing alone on an issue, but he never backed down when he believed in something. Rather than being intimidated, a confrontation seemed to invigorate him.

When the extras went on strike during the production schedule of "Highway," Michael continued to pay them the customary union salary, but promised to abide by whatever pay increase their new Guild contract might provide. When the strike was settled, members representing the Screen Extras Guild visited the set to thank him. He was gracious, but he wasn't looking for thanks. He believed in being fair and sharing the benefits of success with everyone around him. No wonder people vied for positions on his crews when openings occurred.

Transportation coordinator Clyde Harper was with Kent and Michael for years. It's a job that Clyde claims covers just about anything nobody else wants to do. Clyde was on hand when the "Little House on the Prairie" pilot was shooting in a location mired in mud. The rain poured down, flooding the area, and all the heavy equipment trucks were stuck.

Clyde said, "It was like World War II out there, and along comes someone wanting to see the producer. So I looked around for Kent, and there he was driving a big D-9 Caterpillar, pulling trucks out of the mud. I pointed to the Cat and said, 'There he is, Kent McCray, the one driving the big Cat.' This person looked back at me and said, 'the producer's driving a tractor?' I said, 'Sure. And Michael's directing traffic!'"

❖

Gary Wohlleben was Mike's financial watchdog for production costs, and as such spent as many hours in the office as he did on the set. Once Gary's grandmother called from Michigan and Michael happened to be standing next to Gary's desk. He picked up the telephone and, in the unmistakable Landon tones, answered, "Gary Wohlleben's office." In some parts of Michigan that story is still repeated, with emphasis on the high-class stars Gary has answering his office phone.

Dennis Korn works with Jay Eller handling Michael's finances. Dennis, business-like and serious, was devoted to Michael, regarding him as the most special person he's ever known. Dennis recalls that at the National Association of Television Producers and Executives convention in New Orleans, Michael signed autographs for ten hours on the convention floor to promote the syndication of "Highway."

Transportation coordinator Clyde Harper

Dennis Korn with Mike

On a break from their booth, Dennis wandered over to where the Gorgeous Ladies of Wrestling were posing for amateur camera buffs. He asked them if he could get a picture with the girls, even just one girl. He was told no, that he had to be at least a station manager to have that privilege. Dennis was somewhat stung by this rebuff, and he wandered back to his own booth looking disconsolate.

"What's wrong?" Michael asked.

Dennis said he'd been told he wasn't important enough to have his picture taken with the Gorgeous Ladies of Wrestling.

Michael could see that he felt bad. "Okay," Michael said, and marched his confederate back to the GLOW booth.

"Ladies, I need a picture with you," he said.

In no time the girls lined up for a picture.

"Thanks," Michael said, and shoved Dennis into the picture.

They wandered back to their own booth with Dennis holding a treasured snapshot, and Michael whistling with satisfaction.

Casey Peterson co-starred with Michael and Barney Martin in the pilot of Michael's new CBS series, "US." Casey didn't have a lot of experience, but Michael thought he showed great promise. When casting director Susan McCray brought him in, Mike knew right away that he was right for the part.

Casey recalls, "He would help me get through it with laughter, because I was scared to death. My first big chance. If a scene seemed too awesome and I was having trouble, he'd say something like, 'Give up that USC acting crap. I wrote the scene, I know it's a stupid scene, just do it.' And I did."

When Barney Martin, a veteran Broadway and television actor, was cast in "US," he was the envy of his acting friends, who told him, "You'll have a huge motor home as a dressing room." When Barney got to the location on the first night, assistant director Jack Willingham sent him to the honey wagon, a huge truck with restrooms and small dressing room cubicles for the actors. Barney walked slowly toward his own little cubicle with a nameplate on it, wondering where the motor homes were kept. He felt better when he noticed that the one next to his had a "Michael Landon" nameplate on it. Michael never had a star's personal motor home on any show, because he felt everyone in the company was equally important.

Barney says, "That's what made it such fun to work with them. I never found anything like that atmosphere anywhere else."

Barney Martin, Casey Peterson, and Landon, the
three generations starring in the 1991 "US" pilot

Landon with Matt Labyorteaux

Pat Labyorteaux, Matt's brother, with
Merlin Olsen, who played his father

While he was sick, Michael talked with both Casey and Barney about how sad he was "US" might not go on. His sadness was truthfully more for them than for himself.

Michael Donaldson was Michael's attorney for the past eight years and a friend before that. He was always impressed by Michael's quick grasp of legal principals, but more impressed with his love of children. He asked him once, "You really love kids, don't you?" and Michael grew serious for a rare moment.

"Yes," he answered, "They don't know who I am." Being a star was never totally comfortable for Michael, but with kids he could always be himself.

❖

Matt Labyorteaux played Michael's son, Albert Ingalls, on "Little House" for six years and says, "He treated me like an equal. That can make an eight-year-old kid feel pretty special." He recalled a Halloween when he and Melissa Gilbert and several of the "Little House" kids were trick-or-treating around the motel on their Sonora location. Mike suggested they go to the cemetery, if they weren't too scared. That was all they needed, and off they went to the little graveyard up the hill behind the motel.

"Naturally, Mike had it all set up," Matt smiles. "If it was anything to do with kids, he was part of it. So we all went up the hill and started walking through the gate of the cemetery. It had been there a long time, and wasn't that well-kept, and it was especially spooky on a cold, October evening."

They made it about ten steps into the graveyard when Kent McCray, wearing a bed sheet and lying behind a tombstone, sat up suddenly and gave a loud, blood-curdling yell. "We were back in that motel in seconds," says Matt, "and Michael acted like it was a big surprise to him."

Matt's brother, Pat Labyorteaux, played Andy Garvey on "Little House." He shared the same loving respect for Michael, who encouraged Pat to eventually get into writing and producing. Pat remembers, "standing around the graveyard at a funeral scene trying to look sad, when Mike sidled up and said to me, 'You know, he died on his honeymoon.' Hearing that silly line in the middle of a super-serious scene had me fighting the giggles for the rest of the afternoon."

❖

The child actors in his productions weren't the only kids who loved Michael. Ian Pearl is a Florida teenager who must use a wheelchair to get around. Nevertheless, Ian is a very outgoing youngster and active in school affairs. He wrote a terrific letter to

Michael, who was so impressed with Ian that when the teenager came to the coast to visit, he and his folks were invited to Landon's office to chat. Ian expressed a lot of ideas that appealed to Michael. In turn, Ian thought Michael was one of the most thoughtful, caring people he'd ever known because he listened with obvious interest.

Indeed, Landon did listen closely to Ian and to other people he met who were physically disabled, and translated their experiences into television episodes that accurately reflected the challenges they faced in life.

"The Loneliest Runner" dramatized Michael's own bouts with bedwetting as a youngster, a very sensitive issue and an unlikely choice of subject matter for television. The 1976 NBC production dealt with the shame he experienced when his mother hung the sheets out to dry where the neighbors could see them. It's astonishing that bedwetting was the only problem he suffered as a youth considering the physical and psychological pain his emotionally unstable mother inflicted on him. But Michael attacked the humiliation and agonizing memories of it as he did everything else in his life—head-on. He gave millions of sensitive youngsters, who were similarly troubled, hope that there was a remedy for the affliction and that life would go on.

Location manager John Warren has a child with Down's syndrome and heads an organization of Down's parents. The only favor he ever asked of Michael was help in promoting the Down's group. Michael, with his known love of kids, responded eagerly. Michael and John would travel to conventions of Down's parents from time to time, and John learned an interesting aspect of the star's personality.

"We'd be in a strange hotel in a strange city, and when the mayor or the local station owner invited us to dinner, Mike would often beg off. However, he'd speak to some couple in the hotel who wanted an autograph, and he'd ask them to come along and have dinner with us. We'd end up having dinner with strangers instead of VIP's. That's just the way he liked it."

Michael was always on tap to do public service announcements for causes that he believed in. One of the organizations he assisted was Women Against Rape, a small group in Collingswood, New Jersey, his home town. One afternoon when "Highway" wrapped early on the sound stage, he filmed a thirty-second promotional spot for them. Editor Marvin Coil pulled it from the dailies the following day, and the piece of film was sent to the group's leader, Joan McKenna.

Some time later, Michael learned that his thirty-second PSA had been so successful that Joan's volunteer group was growing into nationwide prominence.

John Warren with Landon and Michael Landon, Jr.

Joan McKenna of Women Against Rape presents award to Landon

Later, when Michael made a promotional trip for the syndication of "Highway," he stopped in Collingswood to receive honors from the group he had helped foster. Joan remembers that when he arrived, "He was tired. He'd been doing promotional visits across the country, but he showed up in a pouring rain and was as bright as sunshine."

After Michael visited the group's headquarters and received an award from civic leaders, Joan recalls that "he sat in a corner the rest of the evening talking with a man who had been a janitor at his high school thirty years earlier."

One of the most difficult responsibilities Michael took upon himself when he starred as Jonathan Smith, the earthbound angel in "Highway," was meeting the sick children who wanted to visit the set. According to writer Dan Gordon, those visits depressed him. Nevertheless, he always welcomed the children sent by the Make-a-Wish Foundation, the Starlight Foundation, or one of the other major organizations that provided terminally ill children with their final wishes.

There were standing orders to stop everything when one of these children visited the set, and Michael spent real time talking with each child alone. Most of the youngsters wanted to visit with "the angel" and ask him what it would be like when their time came to die. Michael reassured them, and they all left happier than when they arrived.

Juliette McGrew, a writer who had interviewed Michael several times, had a son named Hal with leukemia. As the boy's white blood count fell dangerously low, Michael telephoned him.

Michael chatted with Hal in his hospital bed about the boy's desire to be a stand-up comedian some day. His blood count almost seemed to go up as they were speaking. Michael promised that when Hal got better he would call Johnny Carson and ask for an audition with his talent bookers. Afterward, Hal told everyone in the hospital about his conversation with Michael. Hal was soon out of the hospital and spent the next month imagining the possibilities of a career as a comedian. Sadly the dream ended too soon, and Hal never got to meet with the "Tonight Show" talent coordinator. But that extra month of life was a gift from Michael.

In the second season of "Highway" Michael started off with a two-part show that broke a lot of new ground. It was about a youngster with cancer who went to a summer camp for kids with that life-threatening disease. Having Michael Landon and a film

Landon was impressed with ideas for stories sent to him by Ian Pearl, a Florida teenager who must use a wheelchair for mobility

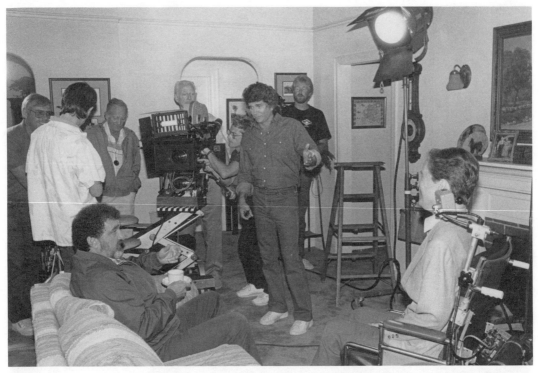

Crew on location with Landon, Victor French, and physically disabled actor James Troesh, who uses an electric wheelchair

Landon on location at Camp Ronald McDonald for Good Times filming a show about children with cancer. Josh Wood, center, wearing eyeglasses, played a major role. He credits overcoming his stutter to his acting stint in the episode. Cinematographer Teddy Voightlander helps Mike line up the shot.

crew in their midst at summer camp was an extraordinary event for the children. Michael used several youngsters, who were very ill at the time, as extras. It was a thrill of a lifetime for them.

During the filming, there was a positive, upbeat feeling on location. Many of the youngsters took on new energy, a new lease on life, from the special attention they received from cast and crew. Michael was far from sentimental about it all. He kidded the youngsters with cancer just as he always did the regular actors on the show, and he had a way of making them feel like part of the real world again. The smiles and laughs were genuine.

One of the kids with a major part was Josh Wood. "It was a really big thing for me, being with a star like Michael. He was funny and never lost his sense of humor. While we were shooting a big scene in the camp dining room, he and Victor French started a food fight that got totally out of hand."

Josh had acquired a pronounced stutter when he became ill with cancer. When his cancer was cured, the speech impediment remained. Although Josh was perfect for the role, those around Michael were concerned about Josh's ability to speak his lines. Mike knew he could do it. Sure enough, Josh not only did brilliantly in the part, but the acting helped rid him of his stutter.

Michael was a great dad, too, and his humor was as much in evidence at home as anywhere else. His oldest son, Mark, remembers a car he had that was always the victim of bad luck. "People would back into me, by mistake. I would get bumped by a hit and run driver, then back into something the next day. The car was a wreck."

His dad explained the problem: "Mark, there are so many dents in that thing, people run into it because they think they ought to!"

Mark's sister Cheryl recalls her father making it a point to shake hands with all her teenage suitors. She was impressed with his thoughtfulness, but her boyfriends began complaining of sore hands afterwards. Cheryl suggested to Mike that he was squeezing too hard.

"Of course," he explained, "I want them to know who they're dealing with."

❖

Columnist Army Archerd has reported on Hollywood's goings and comings for almost forty years. He often met Michael at functions and visited him on the set. "I'll

Mike was a great dad. Michael Jr. gets appropriate head gear when he was cast in the new version of "Bonanza." Mike's laughing because he doesn't have to ride a horse.

Family man Michael Landon with wife Cindy, daughter Jennifer, and son Sean

tell you how perfect he was," Army recalls. "At the height of his career, when he was totally busy and committed to his work, one of my children asked him to speak to their Sunday school class. Michael took the time to do it. That's a friend."

Once Michael's diagnosis had been announced, Army called him every day. That's also a friend.

❖

Betty White recalls that when she was doing her show "Pet Set," several years ago, she found out the morning of the show that Raymond Burr, who was set to guest with her, was unable to appear. In desperation, she called Michael and told him her plight. He not only showed up, but, "with his quick mind and that laugh of his, he gave us one of our best shows ever." She adds, "Thanks, Mike, I still owe you one."

❖

When a particular "Highway" episode pleased President and Mrs. Ronald Reagan, they would call him from the White House. One night, when an episode starring Robert Culp made a strong stand against drug abuse, the Reagans called the Landon home and Nancy talked with Michael about how much she and the president had been touched by the episode.

When Michael was diagnosed with cancer, Nancy called him again. During the conversation she was moved to tears, and Michael attempted to make her feel better. "Nancy, come on, now. It's going to be all right."

❖

One day when they were filming "Little House" at the old MGM studios, a camera man from the adjacent sound stage dropped by and asked to speak to Michael. As an eight-year-old child, the camera man's wife, Julie, had once visited the set of "Bonanza," and Michael had seated the little girl on his horse. The experience remained a highlight of Julie's childhood. Now, years later, the camera man wanted to bring his wife to the set to watch Michael film. Michael nodded assent, but with one condition: don't tell her we talked.

Soon afterward, the camera man brought Julie to the set to watch Michael at work. For a good half hour, while Michael directed the episode, he would stop and stare in Julie's direction. Suddenly he stopped, walked toward her, and held out his hand: "Julie, how are you? I haven't seen you since you were eight years old!" The woman, now in her twenties, was utterly convinced that he had remembered her as a little girl—and maybe he did!

Michael directed an episode of "Highway," in which Dick Van Dyke played a street person who tried to bring joy to others through a puppet. Van Dyke was superb in the characterization, and it was a very moving performance. In the end, the man is killed in a robbery, and Dick played the death scene beautifully. However, the camera continued rolling, and rolling, and rolling. It seemed strange, because this was no time for a prank. Eventually, the first assistant, Maury Dexter, said "cut," very quietly, and everyone moved about. Michael had become so involved with the scene that he was in tears and couldn't give the command to cut the camera. His respect for Van Dyke was immense, and the feeling was mutual. "What an incredible human being," Dick remembered.

Lew Ayres worked with Michael several times over a period of thirty years, and was one of Landon's favorites. On one occasion, Lew played a writer in an episode of "Highway" shot on location in Morro Bay, California. Usually a shimmering ocean resort, Morro Bay was drenched with rain for several days. On the final day of the shoot, Lew was scheduled to film the scene in which he goes to sea in a boat and disappears. The sky cleared and the weather was perfect—"Landonluck," Mike called it. "He was without equal," Lew remembers, "an inspiration to do your best at all times."

Oscar-winning actress Patricia Neal was offered a role in a "Little House" episode about a woman whose fatal illness forces her to find a home for her three children so they will be together after she's gone. When she got the script she discovered that the shooting date conflicted with her family's annual vacation in Norway that had already been planned. She asked her agent, the incomparable Irving "Swifty" Lazar, what she should do.

"Go to Norway," he said. "Turn the part down."

"Couldn't you ask Mr. Landon if he would delay it?" Neal wondered.

"No," said Lazar, "Turn it down." Patricia couldn't bear to turn the role down, and she called Michael at Paramount. She explained the problem and Michael was

Landon with Dick Van Dyke and friend

Landon with veteran actor Lew Ayres and Matt Labyorteaux

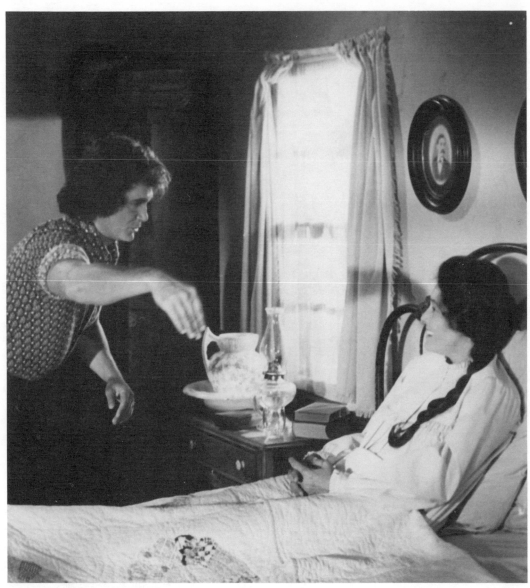

Landon directing Patricia Neal

very understanding. He told her he'd see what he could do and would talk with her agent. The following day Lazar called her back.

"They're delaying it two weeks," he told her. She was elated.

Landon was delighted to have Patricia Neal play the role, and he wrote a touching poem that was read at her character's funeral in the episode.

At Landon's funeral service, Melissa Gilbert Brinkman read the poem, which seemed to sum up Michael's own feelings about himself:

> *"Remember me with smiles and laughter,*
> *for that is how I will remember you all.*
> *If you can only remember me with tears,*
> *then don't remember me at all."*

Laughter

On May 9, 1991, Michael appeared on Johnny Carson's "Tonight Show." Michael felt that since he looked and felt well, it was only fair that he show his friends that he was still hanging in there. He also wanted to make a statement about the tabloids that had whipsawed him with tales full of medical misinformation and negative prognostications. He wanted a chance to make a comment that everyone would see, and to express his feelings about their "inside stories" riddled with falsehoods.

Johnny and Michael had been friends for a long time, and Mike had been one of Carson's guests in the early days of the NBC show.

"We were both products of television," Johnny recalled. "We understood each other. I don't think either of us took ourselves all that seriously."

Johnny and his wife Alex had been invited to Michael's fiftieth birthday party; everyone had dressed in fifties garb. As they were driving to Michael's Malibu ranch, Alex had wondered aloud if there would be a lot of Hollywood celebrities there.

"No, I don't think so," Johnny remembers answering. "It'll just be people he cares about—family, friends, people he works with." And he was right. Johnny, Michael, Victor French, and Brian Keith were the only stars there. Michael just wasn't a Hollywood type.

The May 9th show turned out to be Landon's last television appearance, and it was the second highest rated "Tonight Show" in its history. Film clips from the show were run on news broadcasts, and photographs appeared worldwide.

That night the two men discussed a recent dinner at a favorite Malibu restaurant, Beau Rivage. As they left, Johnny accidentally backed his car over the old cat that belonged to the owner, Daniel Forge. According to Daniel, "The cat screeched, but took off and we couldn't find her. I told the Carsons not to worry, that I would take care of the cat, and they left."

Within a few weeks of the dinner, Michael guested on the "Tonight Show," and he told Johnny that the cat had died. It caused Johnny great pain, until Michael laughed and admitted that the cat was fine.

Later, they all dined once again at Beau Rivage. Mike's producer, Kent McCray, had gotten a copy of the menu and made a few substitutions. As Johnny read the menu, Michael kept a straight face. It was some time before Johnny noticed the special feline items added to the menu, such as "Pussy Mousse, à la Mercedes...prepared right on the property." Johnny roared. One more for Michael.

Landon and Johnny Carson

Merlin Olsen was an all-Pro defensive lineman who played for fifteen years in the NFL. When he got out of football he turned to acting, and one of his first jobs was on "Little House." Michael wanted to give him something easy to do his first day on the set. Olsen was new to acting, and Mike thought he'd ease him into it.

~ Appetizers ~

PLEASE NO PIPE or CIGAR SMOKING!!

Carpaccio Venezia 8.25
Thin raw beef, capers, minced onions, mustard Parmesan

Baked Filet of Feline ... 8.75
Declawed, deep fried ——— served on a bed of sand

Escargots Positano 8.75
In pasta shell, garlic butter, tomato concassee

Tureen of Tabby ——— 8.75
Scallions, tomatoes, cucumber — in 30 wt. oil

Mouclade au Curry ——— 9.25
Fresh mussells, curry sauce, apples. cream.

Scampi alla Livornese . 12.00
Sauted in; Olive Oil, garlic, white wine, basil.

Mozzarella Genovese or Napoletana . 6.00
Parsleyed anchovy butter or Marinara.

Fresh Servuga Molossol Caviar according to market price
Served on buttered fried toast with all the trimmings
also fresh Beluga available on two days notice, accord market price.

Soups & Potages
Our Special Chilled California Soup 5.50

Soup du Jour (ask your waiter to check the parking lot)

6% Sales taxes will be added to all taxable items. We are not responsible for lost or stolen items. We reserve the right to refuse service to anyone.

~ Salads ~

Dinner Salad House Dressing ----- 4.00
Greens, tomato, String beans, Julienne of beets

Imported Roquefort cheese dressing ... 2.50

Insalata Tricolore 7.75
Belgian endive, avocado, water cress, radicchio, chutney dressing

Pussy Mousse a la Mercedes
prepared right on the property ----- 5.75

~ Pastas ~ (Entrée)

Fettuccine Luciana. Parmesan, cream, egg yolk 11.00

Linguine Pesto. Sweet basil, pine nuts, garlic, olive oil. 12.00

Kitten Carson with Macadam sauce 11.00

Linguine Pollo. Smoked chicken, mushrooms ----- 15.50

Linguine Pescatore. Seaweed pasta, clams, mussels ... 17.75

~ Entrées ~

White Fish Belle Meunière 17.50

Pressed Pussy Provencale. served outside in the dark 17.50

Suprême of Chicken Monte Christo . 15.00

Roast Duckling Mirabelle ----- 17.25

Veal Piccatta Lemon Butter ——— 18.50

Veal Beaurivage. cream, Wine, garden herbs 19.25

Filet Mignon Sauce Trois Moutardes . 21.50

Baby Lamb Chops Tarragon Sauce 22.50

A CHARGE OF $2.50 WILL BE APPLIED ON ALL SPLIT ENTREES.

"He wanted to help calm my nerves," Merlin recalls, "but that was almost impossible that first day."

Michael set up an animal shot—always fun—for Merlin's plunge into an actor's life. A crow was supposed to land on Merlin's head. "It would have been so simple," maintains Merlin, "except that the darn crow wouldn't land. He kept flying off." Michael retrieved the bird several times himself, and finally, after some rehearsal, thought everything was settled. Everyone knew what they were supposed to do.

The trainer placed some meat on Merlin's head, the cameras rolled, and sure enough the crow landed. But in grabbing the meat, the bird scratched Merlin's head worse than he'd ever had it scratched by opposing linemen in the NFL. Adding insult to injury, the bird took an extra moment to relieve himself in Merlin's hair before flying off.

"Well, it certainly introduced me to the show. And from there it could only get better. Michael always had that wild sense of comedy."

In another episode, Merlin was wrestling with a big, rugged character actor, Leo Gordon, who was showing strain after some of the wrestling scenes. Merlin mentioned it to Michael.

"That's okay," Mike assured him, "Leo dies in the next scene anyway."

Though the unexpected reply got a huge laugh from Merlin, Michael immediately went to the stunt coordinator and made sure Leo would not get involved in any more heavy physical action. With all the black humor, Michael was always very caring of his actors.

❖

On "Little House," Moses Gunn played a newly-arrived resident of Walnut Grove that Pa Ingalls was trying to get into the local church. The congregation had never had a "person of color" before, and it took some arguing for Pa to talk the more reluctant members into accepting this new man into the fold.

When they were ready to shoot the scene where church members arrive at Moses' house to tell him the congregation has voted him in, Mike went to elaborate lengths to make sure the actor didn't miss out on a Landon ribbing. Michael knocked on the cabin door and Moses was given the cue to open it—and he did. Standing there in white robes and hoods were Merlin Olsen and Mike, who was holding a huge black whip.

"You lost," announced the giggling Landon, and Moses fell on the floor laughing.

Merlin Olsen, Mike's good friend

Moses Gunn, who guest starred on "Little House" and went on to star in "Father Murphy," talks with Landon and Keenan Wynn on a "Highway" location in Tuscon, Arizona

Michael with Helen Hayes, who guest-starred in the first episode of "Highway"

Landon with Brandon Tartikoff

Moses Gunn moved on from "Little House" to star in Michael's next series, "Father Murphy." It wasn't exactly a tough negotiation for either party.

"When I finished "Little House," Michael said, 'Moses, when you go home I'm gonna send you this script.' " That was it. Moses, Merlin, and young Timmy Gibbs became the stars of "Father Murphy" in an almost casual way. But that was how Michael liked to do things. "He knew how to handle people," Moses said.

When Timothy Gibbs, who played Will on "Father Murphy" brought his parents, Ray and Paula Gibbs, to the set on the Tuscon, Arizona location, the young actor was new to the series and wasn't well acquainted with Landon.

Timmy went up to Michael and said, "Mr. Landon, these are my parents."

The executive producer of their son's television series smiled, stuck out his hand—and then his tongue, on which sat a lizard.

The Gibbs were caught completely off guard by the antic behavior. "They figured I was going to have a pretty good time when they saw that," Timmy says. "Boy, were they right!"

❖

In June 1989, NBC honored four of their longest-running network stars at an affiliates' meeting in Washington, D.C. Special awards were given to Bill Cosby, Milton Berle, Bob Hope, and Michael Landon in honor of their many years of success at NBC.

First class was overbooked on the flight back to Los Angeles, so NBC honcho Brandon Tartikoff volunteered to sit in the coach section. He had worked hard during the affiliate's meeting—in fact, Brandon works hard all the time—and he fell asleep almost as soon as the plane took off.

In his usual playful mood, Mike donned a flight attendant's apron and earrings, put on some of her lipstick and fluffed up his own luxuriant long hair. Looking like a *Mad* magazine-version of a stewardess, Landon headed back to coach to awaken the network chief and offer him a meal.

When Michael later asked Brandon what he thought of that stewardess, Tartikoff deadpanned, "I thought she looked kind of ugly."

When he believed in something Mike could be a tiger. Brandon Tartikoff, whom Mike respected more than most network executives, suggested he try a different subject than senior citizens for the "Highway to Heaven" pilot. Michael didn't, he believed in the story, and marketing tests eventually proved him right. When the pilot aired, his opening night rating was a whopper and the show ranked third for the week. Helen

Hayes was the guest star and remembers the experience with great pleasure. "He was wonderful to work with, just wonderful."

❖

Mike accepted Bob Hope's invitation to appear on his birthday special, but he was apprehensive about what Rapid Robert might want him to do. He found out fast that Hope and his staff had no intention of letting him play a cowboy or an angel, something Landon fans were used to. Dressed as a punk rocker with spiked hair and a leather jacket, Michael and lithesome Brooke Shields did a song and dance number. Michael, who couldn't sing or dance, took on the challenge.

Punk rocker Mike sings for Hope

The dance steps were tough to master, and no matter how hard Brooke and Michael rehearsed, they weren't in sync. Finally, Michael said to Brooke, "Let's wing it," and it worked.

What did Brooke have to say about her punk dancing partner? "...I wish I could have been one of his children!"

Director/"Angel" Landon with heavenly
assignment supervisor Bob Hope

Now that Michael had made an appearance on Bob Hope's show, the fabulous funnyman owed Landon a guest shot. Michael came up with a classic spot for Hope on "Highway," in which he would play the heavenly assignment supervisor, who was always having computer trouble and misplacing his earthbound angels. The role was perfect; Hope loved it.

The sequence required Hope to assign a tough problem for Michael to unravel as Jonathan Smith, the angel.

"This isn't gonna be easy," Jonathan says. "Any suggestions?"

"You're the angel," says Hope, flapping his huge plastic wings, "Wing it!"

It was vintage Hope. "He had a great sense of humor," Hope says of Landon, "and all that hair!"

Vince Gutierrez is a sound effects editor, who also wrote scripts for Michael, including numerous episodes for "Little House" and "Highway." "Mike wasn't too thrilled with network interference," he remembers. "During the first years of "Little House," one executive was really on his case. She was always on the set, it seemed, asking stupid questions. One afternoon she cornered him and asked point-bank, 'Mr. Landon, what direction are these shows going to take? What direction are you going in, Mr. Landon?' "

He stopped and stared at her. "We're going west."

Then he walked away and never said another word to her. She never returned to the set.

❖

Michael's crew loved him. Why wouldn't they? He never tried to tell anyone how to do his or her job. He appreciated their talent and they appreciated his confidence in them. The crew never left voluntarily. "You either retired or died," said transportation coordinator Clyde Harper.

Michael loved to pull surprises on Mary Yerke, his seasoned script supervisor on "Little House." One day, in the Simi Valley location for the town of "Walnut Grove," he put small stones in the capacious pockets of her director's chair. She had to move it from scene to scene, and as she did, Mike and the crew would add more rocks. By the time the afternoon was ending, Mary was hauling twenty pounds of rocks in her chair pockets.

Another time when Michael was directing, he called Mary to join him near the camera. She walked over, but he beckoned her to come closer...closer...and even closer.

Gary Wohlleben had a very expensive "receptionist"

Landon crew members John Muselman, Eddie Heboian, and Gerry Dery

She bent to hear what he had to say. When Michael opened his mouth, a tiny frog hopped out. Mary almost fainted.

When she died, Mike spoke at her funeral in a glowing tribute to his long-time friend. After the service, another veteran Landon crew member, Johnny Muselman, summed it up for everyone when he came up to Mike with tears in his eyes: "Gee, Mike, you spoke so nice I wished it was me that died."

Michael took great pride in his body and kept himself in wonderful condition throughout his career; therefore, it was mandatory that his stunt men stay in great shape as well. Hal Burton, his stunt double for many years on "Bonanza," was stuffing his face with candy one day as Michael walked by.

Landon tapped him on the belly and cautioned, "You're gonna eat yourself right out of a job."

"Ha!" answered Burton. "That'll be the day. I'm always gonna be this thin."

Later the wily Landon approached the male costumer with a fiendish idea. Every night after work, they would take Burton's jeans in a quarter of an inch.

As the days went by, Hal began to notice he was indeed getting fatter around the waist. Eventually, one morning when it appeared Hal would bleed internally if he buttoned his jeans one more time, Michael started laughing, and let the worried stunt man off the hook. It was obviously a great relief to Hal that it was Landon, and not lard, that had caused his waistline expansion.

Michael told writer Tom Ito that "the public's perception of me is that I'm this goody two-shoes kind of guy." But that was not the case. There was always a sense of mischief just below the surface. He liked to poke fun, and he did it in totally unexpected ways.

NBC publicist Bill Kiley remembers a scene in which Ma Ingalls was sitting on the porch churning butter. Michael hid a speaker in the butter churn, and as Karen Grassle rotated the paddle, Landon's sepulchral voice announced, "I don't know what you're doin' Ma, but it sure feels great." Kiley reports that Karen jumped several feet off her chair before she broke into gales of laughter.

Mike with old friend, NBC publicist Bill Kiley

Mike hugs co-star Karen Grassle who played his wife on "Little House"

Melissa Gilbert with Victor French on location for "Little House"

Mike with two other members of the "Little House" cast, Linwood Boomer and Melissa Sue Anderson

Bill Kiley remembers that during the filming of the pilot for "Little House on the Prairie," Pa and Ma Ingalls were required to dig a trench around their cabin to protect it from an onrushing prairie fire. The camera rolled and Michael and Karen Grassle bent to their jobs.

Shoveling until the sweat was rolling down her forehead, Karen failed to hear Michael whisper "cut" to cinematographer Teddy Voightlander. The dedicated actress went on scooping sand out of the trench for several extra minutes before she realized the crew had stopped filming and was solemnly watching her shovel her little heart out. As soon as she stopped they politely applauded, lead by the chortling Landon.

He pulled a similar trick on Melissa Gilbert one day when she had been directed to walk over a bridge out of town and head toward the prairie. Again Michael said "cut" as quietly as he could and Melissa kept walking down the road—and walking, and walking, and walking! She'd hiked almost a half a mile from the laughing crew before she realized the camera was no longer rolling.

When Pam Roylance joined the show in its final year, she played a scene with Stan Ivar in which she walked away from their conversation in company with Melissa Gilbert.

"Get ready for a long walk," Melissa whispered to a confused Pamela. "You're a newcomer and we'll keep walking forever before they give us the word they've stopped shooting." Pam wanted everyone to be happy with her first episode on the new show, so she and Stan walked away from the camera—and kept walking.

"Melissa was right," Pam recalls. "We walked almost half a mile. The crew was in hysterics, so I had to look surprised. But I knew, and to be honest, it was worth it to earn a place in that wonderful group."

In the early days of "Bonanza," Herm Lewis handled the publicity for NBC on the NBC show. The series was new, and Michael was not the world-wide figure that he soon became. Lewis accompanied Mike on an appearance at the Camp Pendleton Rodeo, at the marine base in San Diego County, California. Prior to the events, Herm and Mike were invited to the officers' club on the base. There was some Indian-wrestling going on in the bar, and Herm was introduced to the young first-lieutenant who had been designated base champion.

Herm was young and feisty then, and he was the lieutenant's equal in all their arm-wrestling matches. The two were attracting everyone's attention in the bar, but soon the focus concentrated on "the actor" with Herm. Michael sauntered over to the table where they were wrestling, and sat down in Herm's spot. The young lieutenant smiled, and the other marines and their ladies gathered 'round. You could see they thought that a Hollywood "pigeon" was about to be defeathered.

"Of course, he beat him. He beat him bad," Herm recalls. "Michael downed the young marine without wrinkling his shirt sleeve." It was a nice moment. A blow for those "Hollywood Cowboys," as Herm put it. For the rest of the evening, the crowd around the bar was much warmer to the visitors from Hollywood. Of such stuff are legends made.

❖

Michael loved practical jokes, and the butt of most of them were his closest friends. Lorne Greene was one of those people very dear to Michael, and Lorne was the victim of some of his wildest stunts.

The "Bonanza" stars were making a personal appearance before an audience of thousands. Lorne was going to end the show with the song, "My Cup Runneth Over," with the band behind him. Lorne was justifiably proud of his singing voice, because it was truly a thing of beauty. But shortly before he went on, the mischievous Landon appeared at his side in the wings.

"Just move around, he'll never be able to hit you," he whispered.

"Hit me?" asked the astonished Lorne.

"There's a sniper out in the crowd, somewhere up on one of those buildings, but they've got him cornered. Just keep moving so he can't get off a good shot."

The now thoroughly undone Lorne edged nervously out onto the stage and spent the next three minutes and forty-two seconds singing and moving like he'd never moved before—from the piano to the band leader, to the wings and back again. The audience must have found it quite a challenge to follow Pa Cartwright as he dodged and weaved across the stage, but Dan Blocker and Michael Landon, watching from the sidelines, were doubled over with laughter.

Lorne's two TV sons were a greater trial to their old man than any real sons might have been.

Dan Blocker, who wanted to show off his new car, drove Michael, Lorne, and his wife Nancy to the top of Pike's Peak to see the view. On the ride down, Michael and Dan were sitting in the front seat and Lorne and Nancy in the back. As they approached the steepest grade of that steep descent, Dan began to pound his foot on the brake pedal, apparently to no avail.

"Now what the hell...?" the massive Blocker whispered.

Lorne heard him. "What?" he asked from the back seat.

"Can't understand it," said Dan, pounding the pedal furiously. Michael sank down in the front seat as if to protect himself, but actually he was trying to keep from laughing. While Dan hurtled down the mountain side, careening around one curve after another as if he had no brakes at all, Lorne and Nancy aged several years in a matter of minutes.

It was several days later before Dan and Michael confessed to that one—and several more days before Lorne stopped shaking.

Lorne and Michael were as close as any father and son. Practical jokes and all, they adored each other. Toward the end of his life, when Lorne lay dying, he called Michael into the room. Michael knelt close to the bed and Lorne raised his hand. Michael grasped it, expecting a last affectionate handshake. Instead, with the little strength left in him, Lorne began their traditional arm wrestling. Michael was filled with laughter and tears at the same time. Lorne had had the last laugh after all.

Bobby Miles was Michael's stunt double on "Bonanza" for ten years. The two were good friends and worked out many intricate routines between them, usually without the guest star who would be involved in the stunt. Such was the case with Charles Bronson. They came to an impasse when Michael was supposed to wrestle a gun from Bronson, who was playing the heavy doubled by Bobby. They couldn't solve the problem.

"Let's ask Charley," Bobby suggested, so they brought the actor to the set.

When Bronson saw Miles with all the pads on under the costume, he was not happy. "You make me look fat," he said. "You can't wear those pads."

"Then you better come up here, Charley," Michael called from the ledge seventeen feet above them. "If you don't like the way Bobby looks, you'll have to do it yourself. I push you off this cliff."

Charley decided Bobby really didn't look that bad after all and the fight went off as planned.

A.C. Lyles recalls that back in 1937 when he was starting out in the mail room at Paramount, the reigning king of the lot, actor Richard Arlen, asked him what time it was. A.C. told him—and with great enthusiasm. A friendship developed and Arlen later bought A.C. a wrist watch, telling the young man, "Someday you'll be a producer on this lot, and I hope you'll use me in your pictures."

A.C. eventually became a Paramount producer, and throughout his long career he never made a picture without finding a part for Richard Arlen. After Arlen died, A.C. included old film clips of Arlen, and if he couldn't find appropriate film, he would mention Arlen's real name somewhere in the script. He never forgot the star's initial kindness to him.

This story was related in a Hollywood newspaper column in the early sixties. Shortly after it appeared, A.C. got a call at his office. It was his friend, young Michael Landon, asking the producer to visit the "Bonanza" set at his earliest convenience for "something important."

When he found the time, Lyles went to stage 17. As he entered, he found Michael, Lorne Greene, and Dan Blocker, all lined up at the stage door waiting for him with their hands outstretched—holding wrist watches!

Doug Friedman, who handles public relations at Genesis, the company that syndicates "Highway," recalls that he met with Michael shortly after the war in Iraq broke out. Michael had just discovered that madman Saddam Hussein had looked upon him as a "father figure" after years of watching "Little House."

"This is great," Mike told Doug. "We have to find a way to get this message to Saddam: that his father figure is a Jew. He'll blow his brains out!"

❖

Nationally syndicated columnist Marilyn Beck wrote about Michael for over thirty years. In the mid-eighties she filmed an interview with Michael at his beautiful home on the beach in the Malibu Colony for a television show she was hosting. On that occasion he told Marilyn a story that has become one of her favorites, and indicates the lengths he would go to in playing practical jokes on close friends.

Michael and Larry Hagman had been friends for many years, and they were neighbors at the beach. Larry was famous in the colony for several major reasons that had nothing to do with his towering success on the show "Dallas." For one thing, it was well known that Hagman did not speak on Sundays. In a feat of self-imposed discipline, he spent every Sunday in silence and refused to break his vow for any reason. Michael, of course, was determined to challenge that rigid rule.

Landon talked a friend into dressing as an Arab sheik, with expensive flowing robes and a burnoose, looking for all the world like a visiting billionaire from one of the Gulf states. On a Sunday, Michael and the phony sheik began walking on the sands in front of the million-dollar homes on the colony beach. The sheik was pointing his hands at house after house, and Michael was nodding, then shaking his head, then nodding. The lavish gesticulating obviously indicated that the sheik was willing to pay big bucks for a place on the beach.

Larry watched the extravagant pantomime and then raced down the beach to ask Michael what was going on. Michael just smiled. Another gotcha!

Larry Hagman, "gotcha" by a sheik

The blind actor-writer-athlete Tom Sullivan had an idea for a show that he wanted Michael to consider for "Highway." Dale St. John, a mutual friend, told Michael about it and, in short order, Mike was shooting Tom's story with Tom in the lead. The episode was about a children's camp for the blind and Tom, as the head counselor, was showing off his athletic prowess. In one scene, Tom had to shoot a basket, not easy for a blind man, even a superb athlete like Tom. But he practiced before the scene and hit five out of eight shots. Tom told Mike he was ready.

"You sure?" Mike asked.

"Piece of cake," Sullivan assured him.

Michael rolled the cameras. First shot, miss. Second shot, miss. Third shot, same. Fourth shot, nothing. Fifth as well. Tom was getting uptight and Michael knew the panic was building. Sixth shot, a miss. Somehow Mike had to relieve the pressure.

Michael started humming. "You know this is starting to cost me a lot of money. They told me not to hire a blind person," Michael said.

The crew could feel it coming and started smiling. Tom got ready for his next try at a basket.

"Deaf, that's what I meant to cast, a deaf person," Michael commented.

"Damn!" shouted Tom. His seventh shot sailed in a beautiful arc and whished through the net.

"Cut," said Michael.

"I didn't know you called 'roll,' " said the camera man.

Tom's face fell.

"Gotcha," said Michael.

And that's the way it went. Regardless of race, color, creed, or physical limitation, you took your share of ribbing.

Tucson, Arizona realtor Ron Janoff has long been a close friend to Michael. At Ron's urging, Michael participated in a Tucson charity tennis tournament for ten years, and raised a great deal of money for local charities. Once when Michael was in Tuscon recording public service announcements for the tournament, Ron held up a cue card in among the others that read "Ron Janoff, realtor." Michael started to read it, then broke up laughing. It became a running gag between them, and Ron did it every year they recorded the spots.

When Michael shot the pilot of "Highway to Heaven" in 1983, several scenes were shot in Tucson, including one exterior scene filmed in front of a senior citizens' home. Michael visited the location the night before the shoot to check with the greensmen

Landon directs actor-writer-athlete Tom Sullivan in an episode of "Highway"

who were planting flowers and shrubs. Everything looked fine and Michael returned to his hotel. The following morning when Landon arrived for the early call, he stepped from his car to see a sign on the lawn, "For sale. Call Ron Janoff realty." Several years later Michael was back on location in Tucson filming at the minor league baseball stadium where the Tucson Toros play. When Michael and Ron went to look at the location that night, Landon said, "I thought you'd probably have a Janoff sign on the infield!"

Ron pointed to the giant electronic scoreboard as the groundskeeper turned on the switch. Michael howled as he read, "This stadium for sale, call Ron Janoff!"

When Ron was in Los Angeles visiting, Michael arranged to meet him for lunch at the Polo Lounge in the Beverly Hills Hotel. Ron got to the restaurant first, and set up his gag. Michael arrived, and Ron followed him into the lounge where Michael asked for a table in his name. The Maitre d' looked down his list and said no table had been booked for "Landon." Michael was furious and insisted he'd made the reservation. Then Ron walked up to the maitre d' and said, "I'm Ron Janoff, from Tucson, and I want a table right away." The Maitre d' led them all to a table with dispatch. Michael was stunned. When he settled into his seat he realized what had happened as he saw the broad grin on Janoff's face.

❖

When Whitey Snyder was asked to do makeup for a television show that "Little Joe" was going to direct, he honestly didn't know who it was. Whitey had done makeup on 467 features since 1940, and didn't know much about TV. However, for the next twenty years he did Mike's makeup.

One time in a Miami hotel lobby, Mike and Cindy were stopped by an older couple who told Mike, "You look a lot younger and better on the screen." Michael laughed and laughed.

"Whitey ought to get a raise," he told Cindy.

A year or so later while after a location shoot in Sonora, California, the company was at the airport waiting for a flight back to Los Angeles. A woman came up to Whitey with her child in tow and said, "Mike Landon looks a lot better in person than he does on TV." Whitey was embarrassed, and didn't know what to think, until he looked across the airport lounge and saw Michael and Cindy watching and laughing their heads off. "He won that one," Whitey says.

Mike with his close friend, Tuscon realtor Ron Janoff, with "for sale" sign in front of the senior citizens' home used in "Highway to Heaven" pilot scene

Mike with Leslie Nielsen and Linda Aldon

When Leslie Nielsen arrived on the set for a guest appearance on "Highway" the first thing he did as he sat in a director's chair was fart. Yes, fart—with the aid of his ever-present "whoopee cushion." With that, he set the tone for the coming week.

The following morning everyone was already very familiar with Leslie's fiendish device, but it was nowhere in evidence. Leslie had forgotten it at home. Michael, however, knew that the episode's writer, Dan Gordon, was visiting the set that day—and that he had been particularly pleased by Nielsen's casting. Michael saw an opportunity too good to miss, and a driver was sent to Leslie's home to get the contraption.

When Dan Gordon arrived and Michael introduced him to Leslie, a loud and embarrassing sound rent the air. Michael turned to Leslie and said, "Very nice, very nice."

Leslie ripped another fart while answering, "Thank you (uggh) Michael."

As they discussed the scene, Leslie asked, "Do you want me to (uggh) speak up in this scene?" Michael could barely contain his laughter.

By now Dan was very uncomfortable, particularly since no one else in the vicinity seemed to be taking any notice. "Dan wrote this script," Michael volunteered.

"And a very sensitive script it is," Leslie answered, as the machine emitted another noisy note.

With that, Michael lost it—and Dan Gordon was introduced to the real Leslie Nielsen.

❖

Birth pains could be intense when a new crew member joined the family. Bill Shotland, a bright, young sound engineer, found his new boss to be wonderful when he first joined the crew on "Highway." Then one awful day when everything they did went wrong, Michael gave him a baleful look. It upset Bill, but what really hurt were the whispers among the rest of the crew.

"Hey, what'd you do to piss the dude off?" (Michael was known as "the curly-headed dude" to cast and crew alike. The mass of his crowning glory may have had something to do with that affectionate soubriquet.)

Bill could find no relief. Fellow sound engineers, Ron Cooper and Hank Brissinger, thought that Bill had "stepped in it," and that Michael was displeased with him. He was beginning to think of packing his bag for a hasty departure from the location, but a day or two later, Michael broke out laughing at Billy's hang-dog look. His initiation was over and Bill was in. The agony had been tense, but the relief was instantaneous and sublime. That was part of the fun of being on a Landon crew, and becoming one of the group was worth the torture.

Bill still took his share of kidding, but some months later he got to be part of a Landon gag. While filming an episode at the El Toro Marine Air Station in Orange County, the crew was kept on their toes by the marine public relations officer who had to make sure the image on the screen met marine requirements. The only real point of disagreement was the length of the haircuts. Marine barbers don't have to be skillful so much as brutal.

All had gone well, but one morning Michael saw that the colonel was once again prowling the set. Bill's hair, like many young men his age, was shoulder length. Michael couldn't resist sending Billy to wardrobe. Within minutes they had Billy dressed as a young marine officer. He walked by the colonel, who was engrossed in conversation with Mike. When he saw Billy, the colonel stiffened.

"Who's that?" he demanded, pointing at Bill.

"Just an extra," Michael informed him calmly.

"He's got to go. The part's got to be recast," the colonel almost shouted.

Then Michael started to laugh. No one, not even a marine colonel, could escape the Landon humor—and the colonel ended up laughing as well.

Mike was always a crowd pleaser, but sometimes the crowds didn't please him. One time while on location with "Highway," camera assistant Bill Sheehan saw how Michael handled an obstreperous fan.

"She was especially large and loud. And she wouldn't shut up. She kept calling Michael's name." The woman was asked to calm down while we shot the scene, but she wouldn't. The security police on location with the company did their best, but they couldn't get her to settle down. "By the middle of the afternoon she'd worked her way right near Michael alongside where the cops were holding people back from the scene. Finally she could contain herself no longer and she broke past Fred Inman, our big motorcycle officer, and confronted Michael."

"Mr. Landon, can I please have a picture with you?" Since he could never refuse a request, Michael nodded and stopped production for a moment while he stood next to her.

"Where's the camera?" he asked her.

"I don't have one," she smiled coyly.

Sound engineer Bill Shotland, the
long-haired, bogus marine, who nearly
gave the colonel a heart attack

Camera operator Mike Minardus in
his extremely expensive Steadicam
rig, of which he is very protective

"I can't supply a camera, hon," Michael told her.

"Then could I have you autograph a picture?"

Michael again nodded. "Sure, let's see the picture."

"I don't have one," she said.

Jack Willingham, the second assistant director brought an eight-by-ten glossy, but didn't have a pen for Michael. He turned to Sheehan, who had a marker in his hand. Sheehan says, "I gave him my marker as he requested, and tried to tell him not to use it. But he wouldn't let me explain." Michael signed the picture and the large lady finally retreated in satisfaction. It was only later that Billy realized why Landon had asked for his marker, and cut off Sheehan's comments. "Camera crew markers are all temporary. As soon as she touches her picture, the signature will rub off. Michael knew that."

❖

Brad Yacobian is an assistant director who worked for Michael for many years. One of his jobs was to make sure everyone arrived on the set on time. When he was young, over-eager, and new to the Landon crew, Brad had noticed that various people were late to the set, and even commented to someone that the boss wasn't in yet. The crew took note. When Michael arrived, Maury Dexter, Brad's boss and first assistant director, called him over. "Brad," he smiled, "here's Mr. Landon. Why don't you tell him your problem."

"Problem? What problem?" asked the boss.

"Well," Brad said, "some people are coming in late."

"Yeah?" asked Mike, aware of the gag going on.

"That's all." Brad tried to get out of the jam he was in.

"But Brad," Maury insisted, "didn't you have something specific to tell Mr. Landon?"

"Uhm...well," Brad stammered, "you were...late...this morning."

As the rest of the crew barely contained their laughter, Michael nodded and turned away, saying to Brad, over his shoulder, "Okay, Brad."

"And everyone would look at you, and grin, and you knew you'd been had," Brad remembers.

On another occasion, he watched a crew member become the target of a far more elaborate prank.

Second assistant director Brad Yacobian with first assistant director Maury Dexter

Mike Minardus, the camera operator on "Highway" often used the Steadicam, a portable camera mount, that allows the operator to do a traveling shot and keep the camera steady. The equipment was very expensive and all of it belonged to Minardus, who was very protective of it. Michael selected one item of this costly gear and had it reproduced by the prop department.

One day Michael was getting angrier and angrier on the set, and Minardus couldn't figure out what was wrong. Michael got so furious that he picked up a piece of camera gear, and threw it to the ground. It shattered in a hundred pieces. Minardus was sick. The look on his face told it all. Then Mike seemed to get even angrier. He picked up one of the smashed pieces, swore at it, threw it into the street and it smashed into a thousand pieces. It was quite a performance, and all for Minardus benefit.

Landon began laughing. It was lucky that he did, because Minardus had had about all he could take. "You had to be tough to be on a Landon crew," Brad says. "Michael and Kent were the very best producers in town to work for, but you had to be tough. Working for Michael was the greatest fun in the world, but it wasn't for sissies."

❖

On the other hand, Michael was quick to stand up for his crew. Dean Wilson, who was property master on both "Little House" and "Highway" remembers an occasion when he had forgotten to bring flash powder for a photographic sequence. He had to mix the ingredients on site, because explosives aren't allowed to be shipped. Once it was prepared, the prop men couldn't be sure how loud it would be, but they knew it would be quite an explosion.

An actor who had recently joined the "Little House" cast was completely unnerved by the loud explosion. He was so rattled that he shouted at Dean, and at everyone else on the crew, and finally complained to Michael. Mike heard him out—how inconsiderate Dean was, what a threat to life and limb that explosion had been, and how dangerous this prop man was that he had hired."

Mike listened to the tirade and then appeared to take a moment to contemplate. Finally he quietly suggested to the actor that he take another look at Dean Wilson, a huge, solidly built, very fit six-footer.

"I wouldn't piss him off," Mike whispered earnestly. "He'll kill you." The actor took Landon at his word and quickly apologized to Dean for the outburst.

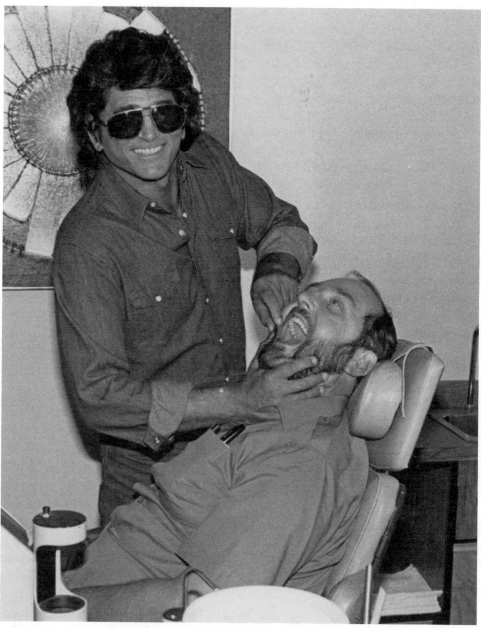

Mike jokes with property master Dean Wilson in a dentist's chair. Dean's flash powder explosion nearly set off one of the actors in "Little House"

For years Jerry Taylor and John Loeffler worked with Michael as editors, and alternated cutting shows under the creative supervision of Mike's long-time friend and post production chief, Marvin Coil. At one time Jerry had an assistant who liked to eat sardines on the job. Marvin tried to discourage it because the fish oil smelled up the editing room. Michael loved to tease Marvin, a founding member of ACE, the honorary editing society in Hollywood, and the only remaining member still actively editing. Marvin likes a neat editing room that doesn't smell like fish," Jerry Taylor recalls, and "he was going nuts trying to get this guy to clean up his act." Michael, upon hearing about it, went to a specialty store near the studio and ordered a case of sardines delivered to the cutting room. Marvin went crazy, until he figured out that it was Mike's gag. Nevertheless, the assistant polished off the fish.

Michael changed a scene in the first script Dan Gordon ever wrote for Michael. It was a scene that Dan really liked. He had no quarrel with the director about this, but he was curious. Why had that scene not made the final draft?

"The scene was perfect," Michael explained, "but David Rose will score this and he'll put violins right there, and when he does you don't need the rest of the dialogue."

Dan nodded in agreement, but wasn't quite sure. When the picture was dubbed, Dan discovered that David Rose had indeed brought in violins and the scene worked.

"Did you ask David about this before you changed it?" Dan asked Mike.

Mike just grinned. "When you work with a guy for twenty-seven years, you know where he's going to put violins."

"Michael knew his business better than anyone else I ever knew," states Dan.

Marvin Coil would agree. Michael became interested in editing when he started directing and the time he spent in the editing room wasn't wasted. "When Michael first started to work on pictures he had directed he would spend a whole weekend in the cutting room. By the end of "Highway" he could take care of most of his problems on the sound stage and cut an hour episode on a Saturday morning."

Marvin was a close friend as well as a trusted associate of Michael's. "When he was in the editing room he was always pleasant and fun, but once we started editing, he was all business. That was when Michael became more serious than I ever saw him, because that's when his creative powers were really coming together. That's when the picture gets made, there in the cutting room. And Michael always wanted it to be the best he could make it."

"Michael was involved in over 800 hours of television, so he probably qualifies as an expert," says Evy Wagner, who worked for him in script development. "He was a genius in story conferences, and could always make a script work. When everyone

The editing crew: Grant Schmitz, Jack Peluso, Jerry Taylor, Anne Hagerman, and Marvin Coil

Assistant to the producer Evy Wagner

else had taken their best shot and it was blocked from all sides, Michael would turn the story just a quarter-turn," Evy recalls, "and suddenly it would all work. He was magic, and very smart."

In 1988, Michael was between films—"Highway" was finished and he hadn't yet started "Where Pigeons Go to Die,"—so he accepted an offer to narrate a special for kids. In "The American Dream Contest," by award-winning producer Arnold Shapiro, youngsters submitted ideas for movies showing why they loved America. They filmed Michael in a meadow with a horse standing nearby, the perfect bucolic setting for the perfect American father image. Except that the horse whinnied, ruining take after take. Michael turned and whinnied back to the horse, as if in conversation, and then explained to the camera crew: "He's all excited, he's never seen a Cartwright before."

❖

One of the great thrills Michael and Victor French shared in the last few years was the ride they both took in a supersonic Navy F-18 Hornet with the Blue Angels aerobatic team. The group was practicing in their winter quarters at El Centro, California, a small naval air station near the Mexican border.

Victor, already in some pain from what later turned out to be inoperable lung cancer, entertained the entire Blue Angels crew by telling stories and signing autographs.

The aircraft—the virtual star of *Top Gun*—is an incredible flying machine that was the mainstay of carrier operations in the Gulf during Operation Desert Storm. It's also a mean ride and both men returned exhilarated from their flights.

Michael went up first. He loved his ride, and got out of the cockpit chattering like a magpie. Finally he stopped himself and asked of no one in particular, "Why am I talking so fast?"

Victor went second, and he, too, returned invigorated. He clowned for the air crews when he landed, falling flat on the concrete as if exhausted. On the drive home, he could talk of nothing but the thrill of flying high with the Blue Angels.

Several nights later, Michael showed his video tape of the ride on the "Tonight Show." Johnny Carson spoke for millions of people when he said, "You do have fun, don't you?" Mike did. Always!

Victor French, Blue Angel pilot, navy Lt. Matt Seamon, and Mike

"Foss," Ruth Foster, with Michael's daughter, Jennifer, in a gigantic prop chair on the set of "Highway to Heaven"

Ruth Foster, known as "Foss," had been a stand-in for the female guest stars on Michael's shows for a long time. One evening, after the day's wrap, she was asked to ride back from location in the horse van, and it hurt her dignity. She told the stunt coordinator that after a hard day of work she did not want to climb into a horse van for the ride home. The following morning, Michael himself showed up at her door and invited her to step out on the motel porch. The limousine used for the guest stars was waiting below. Michael pointed to it. "Yours, Foss, no more horse vans."

"That's why people all loved him," Foss says. "He always cared."

Pamela Flynn, Gene Trindl, and Harry Flynn

Pamela and Harry Flynn operate the Flynn Company, a public relations firm that represented Michael Landon, among other celebrities. Harry Flynn, a Harvard graduate, has been a promotional producer for all three major television networks, and has done publicity for Bob Hope, Carroll O'Connor, Bob Newhart, and Ernest Borgnine. Pamela Flynn has built her career in radio and television programming and promotion. The Flynns live in Los Angeles.

Celebrated Hollywood photographer Gene Trindl has photographed Michael Landon since the days of "Bonanza" through "Little House on the Prairie," "Highway to Heaven," and the 1991 pilot, "US." His photographs have graced more than 200 covers of *TV Guide* and his work has appeared in *LIFE, People, Look, Saturday Evening Post, and Collier's*. He lives in Los Angeles.